Novels for Students, Volume 7

Staff

Series Editor: Deborah A. Stanley.

Contributing Editors: Sara L. Constantakis, Catherine L. Goldstein, Motoko Fujishiro Huthwaite, Arlene M. Johnson, Erin White.

Editorial Technical Specialist: Karen Uchic.

Managing Editor: Joyce Nakamura.

Research: Victoria B. Cariappa, *Research Team Manager*. Andy Malonis, *Research Specialist*. Tamara C. Nott, Tracie A. Richardson, and Cheryl L. Warnock, *Research Associates*. Jeffrey Daniels, *Research Assistant*.

Permissions: Susan M. Trosky, *Permissions Manager*. Maria L. Franklin, *Permissions Specialist*. Sarah Chesney, *Permissions Associate*.

Production: Mary Beth Trimper, *Production Director*. Evi Seoud, *Assistant Production*

Manager. Cindy Range, *Production Assistant*.

Graphic Services: Randy Bassett, *Image Database Supervisor*. Robert Duncan and Michael Logusz, *Imaging Specialists*. Pamela A. Reed, *Photography Coordinator*. Gary Leach, *Macintosh Artist*.

Product Design: Cynthia Baldwin, *Product Design Manager*. Cover Design: Michelle DiMercurio, *Art Director*. Page Design: Pamela A. E. Galbreath, *Senior Art Director*.

Copyright Notice

of this work have added value to the underlying factual material herein through one or more of the following: unique and original selection, coordination, expression, arrangement, and classification of the information. All rights to this publication will be vigorously defended.

ISBN 0-7876-3826-9
ISSN 1094-3552

Printed in the United States of America.
10 9 8 7 6 5 4 3 2 1

Candide

Voltaire 1759

Introduction

François-Marie Arouet, best known under his pen name, Voltaire, is such a historical giant that some scholars, like Ariel and Will Durant, call the eighteenth century the "Age of Voltaire." Voltaire was unrivaled in stature as an author. He criticized everyone and signed his works with "Ecrasez l'infame" or "down with infamy." Though he wrote more than eighty volumes of material, his most popular work remains *Candide; ou L'optimisme, traduit de l'Allemand, de Mr. le Docteur Ralph*, translated in 1759 as *Candide; Or All for the Best*. The reception of the work was controversial; in fact, the Great Council of Geneva immediately denounced it and ordered all copies to be burned.

Candide parodies the philosophy of optimism put forth by Gottfried Wilhelm von Leibnitz. This philosophy states that since God created the world and God is perfect, everything in the world is ultimately perfect. Voltaire had already attacked this philosophy of optimism in his poem on the 1756 Lisbon earthquake. Rousseau answered the poem with a letter, which was leaked to the press, saying it was Voltaire who was mistaken. Voltaire answered back three years later with the tale of Candide. The tale is a fantastic picaresque journey that takes Candide around the world. After he and his friends are killed, they are brought back to life; first rich, then poor; and finally, they wind up on a farm in Turkey.

Author Biography

Voltaire's mother, Marie Marguerite Daumard, was the daughter of a member of Parliament and sister of the comptroller general of the royal guard. She had access to the court of the Sun King, Louis XIV. Daumard married François Aruoet, an affluent attorney, investor, and friend of the poet Nicolas Boileau, dramatist Pierre Corneille, and the courtesan Ninon de Lenclos. The Arouets had five children; the youngest one, born in Paris on November 21, 1694, was Voltaire.

At the age of 10, Voltaire entered the Jesuit College of Louis-le-Grand on the Left Bank of Paris. Voltaire graduated in 1711 with every intention of being a writer. His father, however, wanted him to study law.

In 1713, Voltaire was sent to The Hague as page to the French ambassador. Scandalously, he fell in love with Olympe de Noyer (nicknamed "Pimpete") and was summoned home, disinherited, and threatened with exile to the New World. Voltaire surrendered and studied law. His reputation and covert writing, however, caused him to be blamed for two poems critical of the regent, Phillipe d'Orleans, written by Le Brun. As a result, he was imprisoned in the Bastille from 1717 to 1718. There he wrote *Oedipe*, a tragedy, between the lines of books because he was denied paper. After his release, he began calling himself de Voltaire after a nondescript farm he inherited of that name.

In 1722, his father died and Voltaire was free from his control. In the same year, he met his rival, Rousseau, in Brussels. His growing squadron of enemies, spearheaded by the chevalier de Rohan, managed to have him exiled to England in 1726 where he was delighted to meet Englishmen like Jonathan Swift. In 1729, back in France, he regained favor, published *Lettres philosophiques* in 1734, and became royal historiographer.

Voltaire frequented the court of Frederick the Great from 1750 to 1753. Disillusioned with the powerful Prussian, Voltaire settled permanently in Ferney, near the Swiss border, so that he could easily flee from trouble. There, word of the Lisbon earthquake shook his optimism and he wrote the Lisbon poem of 1756 and *Candide* in 1759. Over the next decade, he and his comrades—the philosophes—joined together to try and topple a few columns holding up "l'infame."

Voltaire had many hobbies. He single-handedly made his town, Ferney, a prosperous watch-manufacturing center. He was also concerned with injustice—most famously in the case of Jean Calas, whose innocence he helped to restore. With an authorial claim on some 80 total volumes of writings, he died in May 1778 in Paris, months after a successful showing of *Irene*. His ashes were moved to the Pantheon in 1791.

Plot Summary

Voltaire's *Candide* opens by introducing the honest youth, Candide, a servant in Westphalia to Baron Thunder-ten-tronckh, who may be Candide's uncle. Candide loves the Baron's daughter, Cunégonde, and is the avid student of Pangloss, a philosopher who continuously "proves" Leibniz's belief that this is "the best of all possible worlds." Candide is expelled from Westphalia when the Baron catches him in a romantic embrace with Cunégonde.

Two seemingly friendly men rescue the cold, hungry Candide, then force him to become a soldier for the Bulgars. After being caught leaving the army camp, Candide receives two thousand whiplashes. Before his punishers can grant his re-quest to be killed, however, the Bulgar King passes by and pardons him.

The Bulgar army engages in a terrible battle with the Abar army. Candide wanders through burned towns with butchered people to reach Holland, where he is treated rudely until he meets Jacques, an Anabaptist. Jacques kindly cares for Candide, who soon discovers a beggar with a rotted nose. It is Pangloss, who caught syphilis from the Baron's servant, Paquette. Pangloss tells Candide that Cunégonde was ravished by Bulgar soldiers, then killed. Jacques has Pangloss cured and the three men travel by ship to Lisbon.

When the ship is struck by a storm, Jacques helps a sailor back into the tossed ship but is thrown overboard himself. Candide wants to try to save him, but Pangloss dissuades him. Jacques drowns. After surviving the ship's sinking, Candide and Pangloss are in Lisbon when a devastating earthquake strikes.

In order to prevent further earthquakes, Lisbon authorities hold an auto-da-fé, where sacrificial victims are tortured and burned alive. Candide and Pangloss are chosen for sacrifice. Because of rain, Pangloss is hanged. Candide is flogged, but before he is burned, another earthquake strikes and an old woman leads him away.

The old woman tends his wounds and takes him to a wealthy home where he encounters Cunégonde, still alive. After the Bulgar attack, she was sold to a Jew, Don Issachar, in whose house she now lives. She also caught the attention of the Grand Inquisitor, who shares her with Issachar.

Issachar arrives, and, seeing Candide, attacks him. Candide kills him. The Inquisitor then arrives, and Candide kills him as well. The old woman plans their escape to Cadiz, where Candide displays his military skills and is hired to fight the Jesuits of Paraguay.

Aboard ship, the old woman tells them her riches-to-rags life story, which includes slavery, losing one buttock, constant labor, and travel. Despite repeatedly desiring to kill herself, she asserts that she suffers from humankind's "ridiculous weakness": she is "still in love with life."

They arrive in Buenos Ayres and go see the Governor, who lusts after Cunégonde and proposes to her. The old woman suggests Cunégonde accept his offer, especially after they discover that they are being pursued for the Inquisitor's murder. They warn Candide to escape.

Candide's servant, Cacambo, agrees with the warning and suggests they join forces with the Jesuits. They go see the Colonel Father Provincial, who, to Candide's dismay, is Cunégonde's brother.

When Candide tells the Colonel that he plans to marry Cunégonde, however, the formerly friendly Colonel becomes indignant and strikes him. Candide stabs him then laments his action. Cacambo, thinking rationally, disguises Candide as the Colonel and they escape.

While eating, they see two naked girls being chased by two monkeys nibbling at their buttocks. To save the women, Candide shoots the monkeys. The two girls cry over the fallen monkeys, who, Cacambo realizes, were the girls' lovers. Candide and Cacambo run off but are captured by Oreillons, who are planning to cook them and "have Jesuit" for dinner. Cacambo, who knows their language, talks them out of it by telling them about Candide slaying the Jesuit Colonel.

Candide and Cacambo endure many hardships until they find themselves in Eldorado, an isolated country of gold mud, jeweled stones, and peaceful contentment. Candide decides this must be the place "where everything is for the best," the place that Pangloss described and Candide has never encountered. Though they are in paradise, Candide cannot live without Cunégonde and Cacambo has a "restless spirit," so they leave with gifts of vast riches carried by a hundred red sheep.

After one hundred days, only two sheep remain, but they are still quite rich. They encounter a tortured black slave. Overcome by the man's plight, Candide exclaims that he must renounce Pangloss's optimism. Cacambo asks, "What's optimism?" Candide replies, "It is a mania for saying things are well when one is in hell." Candide sends Cacambo to rescue Cunégonde while he sails for Venice. But Candide is double-crossed by Vanderdendur, a merchant ship captain, who steals Candide's treasure. Embittered, Candide decides to hire the most unfortunate man in the province to accompany him to France. He chooses a poor scholar named Martin.

Candide is better off than Martin because he still possesses some jewels and he still longs for Cunégonde, while Martin, a confirmed pessimist, hopes for nothing. They soon witness a sea battle in which one ship sinks. When Candide happily saves a red sheep from the water, they realize that Vanderdendur has been killed and the treasure lost. Candide and Martin debate philosophy all the way to France. They experience the many corruptions of Paris, then sail to England where they witness an admiral executed for not killing enough enemies.

He serves as an example to other admirals.

They reach Venice but cannot find Cacambo, which does not surprise Martin. Candide attempts to refute Martin's cynicism by pointing to a monk and girl walking happily together. They discover, however, that both of them also are miserable. The woman is Paquette, who is now a prostitute. The man, Brother Giroflé, detests his life as a monk.

Candide and Martin visit Count Pococurante, a wealthy Venetian. Because Pococurante thinks for himself and can find little to please his tastes, Candide thinks him a genius.

Candide and Martin dine with six strangers, all of whom are deposed kings. Cacambo is the slave of one king, and he helps Candide and Martin sail to Constantinople, where they will find Cunégonde, who is now a slave. Candide buys Cacambo's freedom. While aboard ship, they discover that two of the galley slaves are Pangloss and Cunégonde's brother. Candide buys their freedom and they join him. Pangloss asserts that he still holds to his optimistic views, but mainly because it would be improper for a philosopher to recant and because Leibniz cannot be wrong.

They find Cunégonde, who has become horribly ugly, though she does not know it. Candide ransoms her and the old woman. He also agrees to keep his word and marry Cunégonde. The Baron stubbornly refuses to allow it, however, because of Candide's genealogy.

Though he no longer wants to marry

Cunégonde, Candide is angered by the Baron's arrogance and, without Cunégonde's knowledge, the group ships the Baron to Rome. Candide then buys a small farm where they all live, dissatisfied. They wonder which is worse, their previous tortures or the boredom of the farm. Paquette and Brother Giroflé, both destitute, arrive. After visiting a rude dervish philosopher, who tells them God is indifferent to their troubles, the group encounters a Turkish farmer who treats them kindly. He tells them that his family's work "keeps us from those three great evils, boredom, vice, and poverty." They all agree that this is a sensible approach to life, and each assumes a task on the farm. When Pangloss philosophizes about their adventures and fate, "proving" that all has turned out as it should in this "best of all possible worlds," Candide replies that they "must cultivate our garden."

Characters

Cacambo

Cacambo is "a quarter Spanish, born of a half-Indian father in the Tucuman province of Argentina. He had been a choir boy, a sexton, a sailor, a monk, a commercial agent, a soldier and a servant." He is now Candide's beloved valet and traveling companion. They experience Eldorado together. Towards the end, it is Cacambo who arranges for Candide to find Cunégonde again. Cacambo is also the one who does all the work when they first start farming.

Candide

The fantastically naïve young man who is "driven from his earthly paradise" with hard kicks in his backside is Candide. Like Everyman, from the medieval morality play by that name, Candide experiences as much as a man could experience in order to arrive at a well-deserved conclusion regarding the plight of man. He exemplifies the idea of optimism when he reluctantly enters the world and leaves the household of the Baron's castle in Westphalia behind. Westphalia, so Candide was told, is the best of all possible kingdoms. In retrospect, he sees that it had a few problems.

It is suspected that Candide is the bastard

offspring of the Baron's sister and a gentleman of the neighborhood. This ignoble birth is not held over him except when it matters most—marriage to Cunégonde. In the course of his travels he is conscripted, beaten, and robbed. Circumstances make Candide a criminal, "I'm the kindest man in the world, yet I've already killed three men, and two of them were priests!" People take advantage of him especially when they learn about his love for Cunégonde. Consequently, pretenders mislead him and, therefore, he experiences the loss of love many times. During any pause in the excitement, he ponders his predicament and the human condition in terms worthy of the deepest philosopher.

Lady Cunégonde

Cunégonde is Candide's love interest. As a young woman, she sees her family butchered and is passed from man to man. She ends up with Don Issachar, whose advances she is able to adequately handle. He houses her in Lisbon and the Old Woman becomes her maid.

Having caught the eye of the Grand Inquisitor, she is then shared by the two men until rescued by Candide. Cunégonde travels with him to Buenos Aires. There she marries Don Fernando de Ibarra until Cacambo pays her ransom. But instead of reunion with Candide, she is taken by pirates and sold into slavery. When Candide pays for her freedom, she is old, ugly, and washing dishes. However, she ends up a very good pastry cook.

Brother Giroflé

Despite appearing to be a happy Theatine monk, Brother Girofé hates monastic life. His family forced him to enter the monastery so that his elder brother could inherit the family's wealth. He hates his family as a result. He fantasizes about setting fire to the monastery and running away to Turkey. Candide gives him some money and loses his bet with Martin. Brother Giroflé soon spends the money and he and Paquette, who has spent her money, run away to Turkey. There they live on Candide's farm.

Jesuit Baron of Thunder-ten-tronckh

Cunégonde's brother also survives the destruction of Westphalia and the brutal slaying of their parents. The very handsome young Baron is taken in by a Reverend Father and is soon sent to the Father General in Rome. He is made a Jesuit because he is not Spanish and sent to Paraguay. There he works his way up to become a Colonel who is fighting the Spanish troops. He refuses to allow Candide to marry Cunégonde, so Candide runs him through with his sword.

After recovering from Candide's assault, the Baron is captured by the Spanish. He asks to be sent back to Rome, and leaves Rome as a chaplain to the French Ambassador at Constantinople. After being found naked with a Mussulman, he is beaten and sent to the galleys. Candide rescues him. He lives with them in Turkey but when he refuses to allow the marriage again, Candide arranges to have him put back in the galleys.

King of Eldorado

The King of Eldorado is the ideal sovereign with an ideal system of government.

Martin

Candide chooses Martin to be his traveling companion. Martin is a scholar who "had been robbed by his wife, beaten by his son and abandoned by his daughter, who had eloped with a Portuguese [and] had just lost the minor post that had been his only means of support." Martin, accordingly, is cynical and not the least bit optimistic. However, he is a pleasant man and willing conversationalist. Candide enjoys him so much that he never parts with him.

The Negro

Although Candide had several encounters with slavery, none is more memorable than the encounter with the Negro. The Negro is wearing only a pair of short blue trousers and is missing his left leg and his right hand. He symbolizes the brutality of the institution of slavery in the Americas. But also, he conjures up the first Spanish expeditions to the New

World. The Spanish were so desperate for gold that they slowly butchered the Indians when they did not find it.

Old Woman

See Princess of Palestrina

Dr. Pangloss

Dr. Pangloss tutors the baron's son and Candide in metaphysico-theologo-cosmonigology. Pangloss contracts syphilis from Paquette and loses an ear and a nose. Then he is hanged as part of an "Auto da Fé" ("act of faith"), but not properly. The person who takes his body resuscitates him. He winds up in the galley of a slave ship and is freed by Candide. Up to the end, he still professes a belief in optimism.

Paquette

Paquette is the chambermaid of Cunégonde's mother. She gives Pangloss the syphilis she contracted from a Franciscan friar. Her relations with her priestly confessor are the cause of her expulsion from Westphalia. Since then, she has lived the life of a prostitute. She winds up on Candide's farm, having spent the money he gave her.

Pococurante

Candide and Martin visit a Venetian senator named Pococurante. They have heard that he is a man who has "never known sorrow or trouble." They reckon that Pococurante is a wise man who will be able to help them understand such a troubling world. They expect to find a happy man. Indeed, Candide thinks that he is the happiest man he's ever seen because he is content with nothing and seems to be forever in search of contentment and novelty. Martin disagrees and says that for just those reasons, Pococurante is the most miserable wretch alive. Quoting Plato, Martin says that the best stomach is not the one that rejects all food. There is no "pleasure in having no pleasure." Candide sees his friend's logic and counts himself fortunate, yet again, that he has Cunégonde to look forward to.

Princess of Palestrina

The Princess of Palestrina has the body, when young, of the Venus de Medici. She is betrothed to the prince of Massa-Carra, but he is poisoned and dies. Saddened, she goes to her mother's estate near Gaeta. On the way, Barbury pirates attack them and the Princess is raped. Then she and her mother become slaves. When the pirate ship arrives in Morocco, the fifty sons of Emperor Muley Ismael are at war. The Princess witnesses her mother drawn and quartered by four men. The Captain kills anyone who approaches and she survives. She then meets a castrato who once sang in her mother's chapel. He promises to take her back to Italy but instead sells her into slavery in Algiers where she catches the plague. She is sold several more times. Finally, she is a servant in the house of Don Issachar where she serves Cunégonde. Taking a fancy to the lady, she stays with her.

Media Adaptations

- *Candide* was adapted to the stage with a great deal of difficulty. The writing of the stage production took several decades. The basis for the play was created in 1953 by Lillian Hellman and Leonard Bernstein as their reaction to the "Washington Witch Trials" being waged by the House Un-American Activities Committee. Poet Richard Wilbur was the lyricist, though Dorothy Parker contributed to "The Venice Gavotte." Tyrone Guthrie directed the first performance of the play, with sets by Oliver Smith and costumes by Irene Sharaff It opened at the Martin Beck Theater in New York on December 1, 1956, to mixed reviews. The play has been continually rewritten ever since.

Themes

Human Condition

The grand theme of the novel is the human condition. Candide wonders, what is the best way to approach life? In the story, Candide has been educated in the system of optimism. It is all he knows, but if Candide had been a flat enough character to accept optimism, the book would be without hope. Instead, Candide doubts the philosophy of optimism and eventually rejects it.

The quest of Candide centers on whether the doctrine of optimism taught by Dr. Pangloss is true. If it is, optimism must be reconciled with what Candide experiences. The reconciliation is not possible without some absurd postulations. For example, Pangloss says that syphilis "is an indispensable element in the best of worlds, a necessary ingredient, because if Columbus, on an American island, hadn't caught that disease which poisons the source of generations … which often prevents generation … the great goal of nature, we would now have neither chocolate nor cochineal." (Cochineal is a dye made from squishing millions of bodies of a certain insect native to Central and South America. The dye was used, most notoriously, to make the British Army uniforms scarlet red.) The example also shows how the attempt of a philosophical system to explain every single phenomenon leads to ridiculous connections.

Candide doesn't find such incidental and simple explanations for everyday occurrences as interesting or as valid as his big question, "Do you believe that men have always slaughtered each other as they do today, that they've always been liars ... hypocritical and foolish?" To which Martin replies that that is the nature of the human animal. But the point is made that humans have free will, and the discussion moves beyond the realm of optimism. Candide eventually defines optimism as, "a mania for insisting that everything is all right when everything is going wrong."

The only possible defense of optimism is Candide's luck, which is regularly recited as evidence of that philosophy. For example, "if I hadn't been lucky enough to thrust my sword through the body of Lady Cunégonde's brother, I'd surely have been eaten ... instead ... these people showered me with polite kindness as soon as they found out I wasn't a Jesuit." Still, Candide realizes there is no perfection in the world. He realizes this at the end when he finally has everyone he has been looking for together on a farm. By then, his search appears to be in vain.

Topics for Further Study

- Based on the evidence in *Candide*, what does Voltaire know about the world's climate and geography? Are these physical facts related to human customs? Do the best locations and climates contain the best societies? How do humans interact with the natural world in *Candide?*

- Although he is exaggerating human customs, what does the satire reveal about Voltaire's awareness of other cultures? Or, what does Voltaire think about the New World—both its indigenous populations and its colonizers?

- Voltaire's grasp of scientific knowledge is far above the average person's of the time. Based on the book, surmise the extent of the knowledge of the day of anatomy, physics, and chemistry.

- Voltaire subtly attacks the theory of progress. What is that theory, and do we still believe in it? Is it a good belief?

- Why is satire such an effective method of critique? As critiques, why are satires so often categorized as children's books? In the late twentieth century, why is animation the most appropriate medium for satire?

- Doing a little research into Voltaire's hopes for humans, what do you think would most excite or surprise him if he were alive today? What would depress him?

Religion

The old man in Eldorado expresses the most positive view of religion. The people of Eldorado, who always agree with each other, are all priests who don't pray for anything. Instead, "we constantly thank him." The old man's presentation stands opposite to Candide's experience of religion: "You have no monks who teach, argue, rule, plot, and burn people who don't agree with them?" The old man replies, "we'd be mad if we did." Both in the story, and for Voltaire, religion is something between a man and God—not something that lends itself to power dynamics, priests, churches, and inquisitions.

Happiness

Martin and Candide play a game as part of their debate over optimism. They place bets on whether passersby are happy. Candide always bets that they are, and he always loses. Whenever it appears, happiness is unmasked (usually by Martin) as a cover for anger, grief, and discontent. Happiness, it seems, is the method one uses to get through another day of miserable living.

War

The art of war is not a noble art in the novel. Instead, it is a barbaric system governed by its own rules and using its own reason. Candide's experience of war is as a conscripted soldier. That is, he is arrested and forced to fight. War is revealed as a complete waste of resources. One element of war that is constantly evoked is the idea of acting in "accordance with international law." This is an idea we hear a good deal about today. For Voltaire, through Candide, this meant that soldiers had the right to rape every woman, plunder and pilfer every village. "International law" is the excuse for conducting war. The end of war is always the same, as "the ground was strewn with brains and severed arms and legs."

Style

Setting

Taking seriously the old adage that the entire world is a stage, Voltaire employed that idea in his novel. Much the same way science fiction does today, Voltaire placed ideal societies and backward societies in obscure parts of the world. The rest simply needed to be exaggerated. For example, with a few facts about the unexplored mountains of Peru and the legends of golden cities, Voltaire can create a credible Eldorado. Likewise, the lack of knowledge about tribes in the Amazon jungle allows the tale of the cannibalistic Oreillons.

Another element of Voltaire's use of setting is his invocation of the Eden trope. Many writers since the writer of the biblical book Genesis have used the idea of gardens as paradises (or hells) that one finds oneself in and, for some reason, banished from. Candide journeys through a series of such gardens. Each garden has a geographic location and a lesson to be learned. However, the best garden, like the best bed, turns out to be the one Candide makes himself.

Satire

Voltaire chose satire as a way to challenge the cult of optimism that reigned during that time.

While this form of storytelling and literary composition is ancient, its historical form came into being with the Greek author, Aristophanes, and became its own genre with two Roman poets, Horace and Juvenal. Voltaire is a comic satirist. He simply loved humans too much to be tragic. But because he loved them, he tried to help them as much as possible. Through the exposure of man's follies in the insane but fantastic adventure of Candide, his satire is fresh for all time.

Picaresque

The picaresque story originates in Spanish efforts to satirize the chivalric romance. Whereas the romance tells about the ideal knight and his brave adventures, the hero of the picaresque rambles along the highway living by his wits rather than his honest work. Both the knight and the picaresque hero share the motto, "a rolling stone gathers no moss." During the eighteenth century, changing demographics led to a demand for tightly woven, realistic novels. The picaresque became a low form of artistry.

Candide is a picaresque novel. Candide is forced by fate to ramble about the world collecting people and losing them, gaining riches and losing it all. His travels bring him into contact with the workings of the world, but this only makes him more skeptical. Finally, he just stops rambling. So long as he is still and at work—like neither the picaresque hero nor the brave knight—he can find peace of mind.

Historical Context

Lisbon

Lisbon was destroyed by earthquake on the morning of All Saints' Day, November 1, 1755. The six-minute earthquake kills 15,000 people, injures at least that many more, and destroys thirty churches as well as thousands of houses. Despite the sophistication of natural science, the coincidence that Lisbon, a city fervently Catholic, is destroyed on a Catholic feast day—when the pious were at church—gives rise to superstitious speculation.

On November 19, 1500 Pilgrim homes are destroyed by earthquake. Many explanations again explain the disasters in religious terms. Voltaire, out-raged at such stupidity, writes an infamous reaction to the Lisbon earthquake. In response comes a letter from Rousseau, stating that Voltaire is the one who is wrong. Humans are at fault. Had we not left the natural world, or committed the original sins, and lived in cities, the disasters would not have happened. Further, Rousseau argues that Leibnitz is right—in the long run, everything must be for the best in this best of all possible worlds. To believe otherwise is to give into suicidal pessimism.

France

The Enlightenment period in Europe is about

to give way to political revolution. Reason, during this period, is held to be the supreme power with which to challenge the old institutions and superstitions. In Britain, where the church had long been relegated to the role of ceremonial trappings, science and industry were the dynamos of progress. France, on the other hand, is still dominated by the Catholic Church. In addition, France is still under the control of a nearly all-powerful King. The bourgeoisie in France is weak and its numbers few. The majority of people belong to the lower classes and are barely literate, burdened by taxes, and underemployed. France is slowly industrializing and cannot compete with British factories. France needs reform desperately.

In government, various reforms are attempted. The finance minister attempts to overhaul the economic framework of government. It is too painful, however, and Etienne de Silhouette succeeded only in giving us a new word: A silhouette is the reduction of a figure to its simplest form.

Compare & Contrast

- **The Eighteenth Century:** France and Britain are continually fighting to see who will be the number one colonial power. Half of this war effort involves stirring up Indian "allies" to kill each other before the colonists spread into the wilderness.

Today: With the demise of the Soviet Union America stands as the sole superpower.

- **The Eighteenth Century:** The first intentional use of biological agents by a military occurs during King Phillip's War. The British intention ally infect blankets en route to the Indians with smallpox.
  Today: The United States enforces economic sanctions against Iraq because of their suspected development and use of biological weapons.

- **The Eighteenth Century:** General George Washington advocates fighting from behind trees and rocks, ambush style, instead of the traditional parade-style formation.
  Today: Though guerilla warfare is now the style when necessary, fighting strategies today rely heavily on airpower and missile bombardment to soften up the enemy before ground troops move in. The style today seeks to minimize casualties.

- **The Eighteenth Century:** Medical technology is crude, often doing more damage than the original problem. The STD syphilis is the most dangerous disease of the time.

Today: AIDS remains a devastating and deadly virus despite "space age" medical technology.

- **The Eighteenth Century:** Modes of transportation are limited. All entertainment, such as concerts and plays, is live and industrial necessity attracts more and more people into the large cities.

  Today: With cellular phones, computers, and automobiles, people are moving out of the cities and into smaller communities.

Seven Years War

France renewed hostilities with England over the issue of control over North America. Two moves by the British in 1759 effectively conclude the question of America. First, well-equipped British forces and their American and Native-American allies drive the French out of the Lake Champlain region. They even take Duquesne and, consequently, Crown Point Military road is built through Vermont. The second push is more decisive. The British take Niagara. Then, an epic battle occurs upon the Plains of Abraham, just outside the city of Quebec. British General Wolfe beats French General Louis-Joseph Montcalm in a battle that effectively ends the Seven Years War. Both men die as a result of wounds received during the battle.

Critical Overview

The rulers of Geneva expressed their view of *Candide* by burning it. The idea that the authorities in one part of Europe were incensed enough to set the work ablaze was very good publicity. Smugglers, meanwhile, made sure that anyone anywhere in Europe could get a copy of the small work on the black market. In general, that is the history of Voltaire's reception—people either fervently loved him, or they wanted to burn him. Today Voltaire's works are studied as artifacts and for amusement.

Immediate reviews of *Candide* were often defensive. For example, an anonymous review of the work in the *The Gentleman's Magazine and Historical Chronicle*, in May of 1759, defended Leibnitz. The reviewer stated that no less a figure than Alexander Pope, in his *An Essay on Man*, expressed a belief in optimism. Furthermore, wrote the reviewer, it is not possible to disprove this philosophy, for in order to do so, one must intrinsically know every other system. Only then can judgment be passed on our system of civilization. *Candide*, asserted the reviewer, "is an attempt to ridicule the notion that 'all things are for the best,' by representing the calamity of life, artfully aggravated, in a strange light."

In 1791, James Boswell compared *Candide* to Samuel Johnson's *Rasselas*. In his *The Life of*

Samuel Johnson, he wrote, "Voltaire I am afraid, meant only by wanton profaneness to obtain victory over religion, and to discredit the belief of a superintending providence … " Whereas, Samuel Johnson used satire to direct man's hope toward the "eternal" rather than to satisfaction on earth.

In the first half of the nineteenth century, "the born minister of literature," as John Morley dubbed Voltaire, was posthumously winning the race against Rousseau. Gustave Lanson, in his *Voltaire* of 1902, covers the publication history of Voltaire during the 1800s. During a seven-year period (1817–1824), for example, of the 2,159,500 volumes of anti-clerical and anti-royalist writings in Revolutionary France, 75% were written by Voltaire. "But," Lanson wrote, "where Voltaire's influence was immense, obvious, and still persisted is in the fields of journalism, pamphleteering, and all forms of polemical writing. He was the master of militant irony and murderous ridicule." In terms of total book printings and sales, Voltaire remained the most popular writer.

After 1850, however, as the French Republic established itself and bourgeoisie fervor for the revolution waned, so did Voltaire's influence. Lanson summed up Voltaire's influence: "In general, in countries outside of France, to the extent that historical circumstances moved further away from conditions that obtained in France when Voltaire's work first appeared, his influence is not easily discernible except among certain clear-thinking minds at odds with their social groups or in revolt against its demands and prejudices."

Critic Georg Brandes, wrote about Voltaire against the backdrop of WWI. He suggested that the mood of *Candide* was still relevant. This idea of relevancy remains a strong current in Voltaire criticism. In 1960, in *The Art of Writing*, André Maurois wrote that *Candide* said all that can be said on today's topic—the world is absurd. Therefore, "*Candide* was the high-point of Voltaire's art." Partisanship has disappeared and the focus of criticism now trains on the ideas Voltaire had. A. Owen Aldridge, in *Voltaire and the Century of Light*, wrote that "structural analysis does very little to explain the universal appeal of *Candide*. It ranks as one of the masterpieces of European literature, not primarily because of style but because of its realistic portrayal of the human condition."

That does not mean that structural analysis of Voltaire's work is not being done. In fact, it is being done more and more. William F. Bottiglia undertook an analysis entitled, "Candide's Garden." His close textual analysis of "a literary masterpiece risen out of time to timelessness" discusses the possibility of approaching the novel as internally structured or externally structured. He feels the latter is not possible as "*Candide* encompasses all—there is no outside. Thus, those who claim that *Candide* reflects or comments on the times miss the fact that the times are in the book." He also examines Candide's journey as a series of 12 gardens.

Critics like Roland Barthes and Ira O. Wade

have focused on Voltaire's work in context. They often suggest, in the case of *Candide*, that Voltaire was very hypocritical. By critical consensus and in terms of sales, Voltaire will always be cherished and *Candide* will always be read.

Sources

A. Owen Aldridge, in *Voltaire and the Century of Light*, Princeton University Press, 1975.

James Boswell, in *The Life of Samuel Johnson*, J. M. Dent & Sons, Ltd., 1978, pp. 210-11.

William F. Bottiglia, "Candide's Garden," in his *Voltaire: A Collection of Critical Essays*, ed. by W. F. Bottiglia, Prentice-Hall, Inc., 1978, pp. 87-111.

Georg Brandes, in *Voltaire*, Frederick Ungar Publishing Co., 1964.

The Gentleman's Magazine and Historical Chronicle, Vol. XXIX, May, 1759, pp. 233-37.

Nikolai Mikhailovich Karamzin, "A Letter on October 2, 1789," in his *An Account of a Young Russian Gentleman's Tour through Germany, Switzerland, France, and England*, translated by Florence Jonas, Columbia University Press, 1957, pp. 144-50.

Gustave Lanson, in *Voltaire*, John Wiley & Sons, Inc., 1966.

André Maurois, "Voltaire: Novels and Tales" in his *The Art of Writing*, The Bodley Head, 1960, pp. 35-50.

John Morley, in *Voltaire*, Macmillan and Co., 1872.

Further Reading

C. J. Betts, "On the Beginning and Ending of *Candide*," *Modern Language Review*, Vol. 80, 1985, pp. 283-92.

> Betts examines the parallels and oppositions between *Candide*'s opening and closing chapter, contending that the end of the story reverses the beginning.

Moishe Black, "The Place of the Human Body in *Candide*," in *Studies on Voltaire and the Eighteenth Century*, Vol. 278, 1990, pp. 173-85.

> Black argues that Voltaire employs bodily references throughout *Candide* in order to concretize his treatment of violence, philosophy, and sexuality.

William F. Bottiglia, "*Candide*'s Garden," in *Voltaire: A Collection of Critical Essays*, edited by William F. Bottiglia, Prentice-Hall, 1968, pp. 87-111.

> In his assertive and thorough study, Bottiglia holds that the ending of *Candide* affirms that social productivity within one's own limits can lead to both "private contentment and public progress."

Donna Isaacs Dalnekoff, "The Meaning of

Eldorado: Utopia and Satire in *Candide*," in *Studies on Voltaire and the Eighteenth Century*, Vol. 127, 1974, pp. 41-59.

> Dalnekoff examines Voltaire's use of Eldorado to further his satire by offering a utopian counterpoint to the corrupt world. Dalnekoff also believes, however, that Voltaire satirizes Eldorado through mockery and ironic detachment.

Will & Ariel Durant, in *The History of Civilization: The Age of Voltaire*, Simon and Schuster, 1965.

> This series by the historians Will and Ariel Durant synthesizes the width and breadth of Western European history from the dawn of history to the Napoleanic era. Though their rendition of history emphasizes great ideas and great men, it is surprisingly inclusive. The ninth volume is named for Voltaire and, therefore, the eighteenth century is filled in around him.

Josephine Grieder, "Orthodox and Paradox: The Structure of *Candide*," in *The French Review*, Vol. 57, No. 4, March, 1984, pp. 485-92.

> Grieder places *Candide* in the genre of "paradox" literature and asserts that its paradoxes attack rhetorical, logical, sentimental, and psychological orthodoxies.

Patrick Henry, "Sacred and Profane Gardens in *Candide*," in *Studies on Voltaire and the Eighteenth Century*, Vol. 176, 1979, pp. 133-52.

> Employing a mythical point of view derived from Mircea Eliade, Henry examines three gardens in *Candide*, connecting them to Voltaire's theme of time and to the tension between myth and history in the book.

Patrick Henry, "Time in *Candide*," in *Studies in Short Fiction*, Vol. 14, 1977, pp. 86-8.

> In this short article, Henry contends that only when Candide stops looking to the future for fulfillment does he reconcile himself to his situation and live in the present.

Patrick Henry, "Travel in *Candide:* Moving On but Going Nowhere," in *Papers on Language and Literature*, Vol. 13, 1977, pp. 193-97.

> Henry reads the characters' travels in *Candide* as an effort "to attain ultimate permanence in the flux of reality."

Patrick Henry, "War as Play in *Candide*," in *Essays in Arts and Sciences*, Vol. 5, 1976, pp. 65-72.

> Henry analyzes Voltaire's war themes "in light of Johan Huizinga's *Homo Ludens: A Study of the Play Element in Culture*.

Frederick M. Keener, "*Candide:* Structure and

Motivation," in *Studies in Eighteenth-Century Culture*, Vol. 9, 1979, pp. 405-27.

> Keener closely examines the novel's psychological progression, tracing his self-conscious development and scrutiny of his own character.

Manfred Kusch, "The River and the Garden: Basic Spatial Modes in *Candide* and La Nouvelle Heloise," in *The Past as Prologue: Essays to Celebrate the Twenty-Fifth Anniversary of ASECS*, edited by Carla H. Hay and Sydny M. Conger, AMS, 1995, pp. 79-89.

> Kusch analyzes how Voltaire creates a stagnating "closed garden" image of Eldorado by including a river that leads nowhere. He then contrasts this garden with the group's more feasible "open garden" in Constantinople.

James J. Lynch, "Romance Conventions in Voltaire's *Candide*," in *South Atlantic Review*, Vol. 50, No. 1, January, 1985, pp. 35-46.

> Lynch defines Voltaire's "burlesque of the romance tradition by comparing *Candide* to one tradition of seventeenth-century romance, the Heliodoran novel."

Haydn Mason, in *Candide: Optimism Demolished*, Twayne, 1992.

> In this thorough study of *Candide*,

> Mason traces the literary and historical context of the work and offers a reading of Voltaire's treatment of philosophy, character relationships, and form.

Alan R. Pratt, "'People Are Equally Wretched Everywhere': *Candide*, Black Humor and the Existential Absurd," in *Black Humor: Critical Essays*, edited by Alan R. Pratt, Garland, 1993, pp. 181-93.

> Pratt connects Voltaire's use of satiric black humor with the works of contemporary black-humor writers who, like Voltaire, use dark comedy to reflect the world's absurdities.

Gloria M. Russo, "Voltaire and Women," in *French Women and the Age of Enlightenment*, edited by Samia I. Spencer, Indiana University Press, 1984, pp. 285-95.

> Russo investigates gender issues in the Enlightenment in her book. In the chapter on "Voltaire and Women," she tells about the many important women in Voltaire's life and their curious, though platonic, interaction with him.

Arthur Scherr, "Voltaire's 'Candide': A Tale of Women's Equality," in *The Midwest Quarterly*, Vol. 34, No. 3, Spring, 1993, pp. 261-83.

> Scherr contends that *Candide* reveals

the equality and mutual dependence between men and women, as shown through Candide's own reliance on women for happiness.

Mary L. Shanley and Peter G. Stillman, "The Eldorado Episode in Voltaire's *Candide*," in *Eighteenth-Century Life*, Vol. 6, No. 2-3, January-May, 1981, pp. 79-92.

Shanley and Stillman contrast the unattainable ideal of the static Eldorado with the garden image, which represents an appropriate goal for Europeans living in a non-static world.

Renee Waldinger, ed., in *Approaches to Teaching Voltaire's Candide*, Modern Language Association, 1987.

Waldinger's collection contains essays detailing a variety of approaches to *Candide*, including studies of its intellectual ideas, philosophical background, satire, and comedy, among many others.

Lightning Source UK Ltd.
Milton Keynes UK
UKHW02f1338271117
313432UK00006B/603/P